INTRODUCTION

The history of Partick can be divided into:

PARTICK VILLAGE: from earliest times
PARTICK BURGH: from 1852 until 1912
PARTICK DISTRICT: from 1912 until the present day.

The establishment and development of Partick was due to its location on the north bank of the Clyde opposite Govan, which could be reached by ford or by ferry, and on the west bank of the Kelvin where that river joins the Clyde. Both rivers supplied water for drinking, cooking and washing, and the disposal of sewage and refuse. Additionally, with the judicious use of weirs, lades and dams, the Kelvin could produce 60 horse power to operate millwheels.

Partick also lay on the route taken by the Highland drovers when they travelled south to the Glasgow markets, and formed a convenient place to rest before fording the Clyde. But more importantly, it lay on the turnpike road that led from Glasgow - the chief town of the west of Scotland - to Dumbarton, which for a long time was the main port on the Clyde as well as the chief naval base of 16th century Scotland.

Boundaries:

The precise boundaries of Partick have varied through the centuries, and there has often been confusion as to what area it constituted at any one time. James Paterson, whose 'Talk on Old Partick' was recorded in the Old Glasgow Club Transactions for 1930, stated that:

> 'the lands of Partick were part of the old Crown Lands of Scotland and stretched from the Molendinar in the east to beyond Scotstoun in the west on both sides of the Clyde; the lands of Balshagray from Whiteinch to north of Great Western Road formed one of the royal forests for hunting deer; it was from these Crown Lands of Partick that Saint Mungo was granted a site to build his cell, on which still stands the church of Saint Mungo, Glasgow Cathedral.'

In the Govan Charter of Confirmation, John Stewart of Rossland is named as holding 'the office of forester and custodier of the new forest called Park of Partick.' J. Parker Smith was MP for Partick from 1890 to 1894, and author of the foreword to Greenhorne's *History of Partick*. He recalled that his grandfather had purchased Jordanhill in 1800, and the MP remembered shooting partridge and snipe in his youth in grounds that are now covered with streets, houses and the teacher-training college, which suggests that the area was still wooded in the mid-1800s.

But despite these testimonies, Partick appears to have been confined to an area north of the Clyde running from the Kelvin to Yoker by 1500. An extract from the Charters and Rent Rolls dated 1505 contains the following entry:

> 'Partick occupies a pretty large tract of land extending from Yoker to Gilmourhill or Kelvin. Wester Partick consists of the following pendicles [detached portions of a larger territory]: Bertanlug, Yoker, Philipsland and Wryray'.

In his history, Napier says that the name Partick had ceased to be applied to any part of these lands west of Whiteinch or out of Lanarkshire long before 1873 (when his book was published).

In 1587 a Charter of James VI of Scotland granted in feu to Walter Stewart 'the lands and barony of Glasgow and other lands and duties including Over Newtoun, Nether Newtoun, the West Syde of Partik, Hindland, mill of Partik, mill lands of the same, Balshagrie, Partikzaird, Brewlands of Partik, Walkmill of Partik, mills called Archie Lyon's Mylne, meadow of Partik, and the New and Old Parks of Partik.'

By 1800 the village was bounded by the Kelvin to the east, the Clyde to the south, and Dumbarton Road to the north. As Partick developed, it was the western boundary which moved, and in the early 1800s this was situated round about Cow Loan, running down from the north as a continuation of Rab's Road (Peel Street); i.e. close to the present Merkland Street. However, when the stagecoaches were in operation the Partick stage was a good bit farther west at Balshagray Avenue.

With the establishment of the Burgh, the boundaries were extended so that they included Meadowside, Thornwood, Whiteinch, Victoria Park, Broomhill, Partickhill and the southern part of Dowanhill.

The Boundaries as set out at the formation of the Burgh (1852):

West: This boundary was formed by the Whiteinch Burn which ran southwards to the Clyde, west of the present Westland Drive and west of Whiteinch Bowling Club, before crossing at an angle south-eastwards over Dumbarton Road, so excluding Primrose Street from the Burgh. From there it then ran south-west to the Clyde across Connell's ship-yard, enclosing the eastern part of the yard and the bottom of Scotstoun Street within the Burgh. The western boundary also formed the county boundary between Lanarkshire and Renfrewshire, the latter of which encroached on the north side of the Clyde at Scotstoun in those days. This boundary crossed Dumbarton Road at the point where the Whiteinch tram terminus was later established.

South: This was formed by the north bank of the Clyde from the the mouth of the Whiteinch Burn eastwards, to the mouth of the Kelvin.

East: This boundary passed along the middle of the Kelvin from its mouth to just beyond the Prince of Wales Bridge opposite University Avenue. It was altered in 1872 when the grounds on which the University and the Infirmary were erected were annexed by the City of Glasgow.

North: The above boundaries are relatively straightforward as they were formed by running water. However, the northern boundary is rather more complicated because, as the village expanded in that direction, there was no river or burn to form a natural boundary. The first part went from the Kelvin to Byres Road. Starting near the Prince of Wales Bridge, it ran west across Gilmorehill to meet University Avenue at Ashton Lane behind Parkville (Ashton) Road, running alongside this lane to meet with Byres Road just above where the Grosvenor Cinema now stands. Thus the Byres Road end of University Avenue was enclosed within the Burgh, along with Ashton Road and Sutherland Street. Until it was taken down in 1971, the tenement at the corner of University Avenue and Ashton Lane bore the nameplate, UNIVERSITY AVENUE/BURGH OF PARTICK.

After crossing Byres Road, the northern boundary ran on to Hyndland Road where it zigzagged its way across Dowanhill, enclosing the southern part within Partick by travelling along Albion Lane, just north of Albion Street (Downside Road); along Victoria Crescent Lane and then across the north-western corner of the Training College (Notre Dame Primary School) to the junction of Queen's Place with Prince Albert Road. It then ran along this road to Crown Circus Road North. From there the boundary ran to Crow Road. After crossing Hyndland Road, it followed the boundary 'between the lands of Hyndland and the lands of Partickhill,' i.e. between the present Clarence Drive and Turnberry Road, more or less in line with Clarence Lane; then behind Hyndland School to meet Clarence Drive at the railway bridge. Thus a small part of the eastern ends of Airlie Street and Dudley Drive were included within the Burgh, together with the lower part of Clarence Drive from Broomhill Cross to the railway bridge in Clarence Drive. The boundary then ran north along the east side of the railway line to the south-east corner of the grounds of Gartnavel Asylum, before turning west and running to meet Crow Road just north of Jordanhill Railway Station. Here it crossed Crow Road westwards, then ran south of Southbrae Drive to meet the Whiteinch Burn.

Hyndland Road, c.1905

The name Partick:

The meaning of 'Partick' has never been explained satisfactorily. The 1791-99 Statistical Account of Scotland reports: 'from the lands being called in the deed of conveyance *illum particulum terrae* (those small lands) it is easy to account for the name Partick,' but I do not find this very convincing, for such a phrase would have been commonly used on these documents and would surely have given rise to more than one Partick. In addition, some of the many ways of spelling Partick do not bear out such a contention.

Since it was not until the 17th century that spelling started to become standardised, the spelling of Partick changed with time. Until the present spelling was established, the most common forms in use appear to have been Perthec and Partik.

1136:	PERDEYC or PERDYEC	1414:	PERTHNICK
1152:	PERTHIC	1452:	PERTHWYCK-SCOTT
1172:	PERDEHIC	1555:	PERTHWICK
1174:	PERTHEIC	16th c.:	PARTIC
1186:	PERTHEC		

Other spellings include Partik; Partyk; Perthaic; Perthait; Perthik; Pertiq; Pertique and Prewyc. Most commentators use 'Perdeyc', although Napier prefers 'Perdyec'. Early on, Pertnic and Pertneck are found, but these are thought to be mis-transcriptions by scribes mistaking 'h' for 'n'.

In 1505 the Charters and Rent Rolls contain the term Partikzaird and a similar Charter of August 1591 also uses this name; this is followed at a later date by Partik-Zaird. For a time the letters 'Z' and 'Y' were more or less identical in Scots, (e.g. Menzies), and possibly Partik-Zaird meant Partick-Yard (i.e. the mill yard). The Session Records of Govan Parish Church around the 1600s show the spelling 'particke'.

Population:

It was not until the middle of the 1800s that the population of Partick began to increase significantly. This was due to the deepening of the Clyde which, along with the proximity of rich fields of coal and ironstone (a kind of iron ore), led to the establishment of yards building ships made of iron. The result was a large influx of people from all over Scotland, and Ireland.

The populations at different times were as follows:

1820	a little over 1,000
1834	1,842
1841	3,184
1851	5,043, just before becoming a burgh
1861	10,917, doubled in ten years
1871	17,693, nearly doubled
1881	33,962, nearly doubled again
1891	36,538
1896	45,525
1897	47,800
1901	54,274

The census of 1911, taken shortly before Partick village became a Burgh, found the population to be 66,848.

Byres Road, Glasgow

EARLY TIMES

Pre-history:

Though the first recorded mention of Partick discovered so far is dated 1136, there is reason to believe that a village existed prior to that date.

A geological study of Gilmorehill showed the area to be covered to a depth of about 70 feet by boulder-clay brought down by the great ice sheet from the north-west of Scotland. Diggings on the sites of the University and the Western Infirmary in 1868 uncovered six fossil trees like those found in a quarry in Whiteinch Park Fossil Grove. In the grove, a Middle Bronze Age cist cemetery was found above these trees with cinerary urns of the later Stone Age period. The quarry knowe was probably used for burials during the Middle Bronze Age and the urns date to about 1000BC. Close by, a quantity of calcined human bones were found. Could we claim these to have been the first Partickonians?

Fossil Grove, Whiteinch.

The Romans:

In Caledonia, the Romans built a 37 mile defence from the Forth to the Clyde, with a series of forts at two mile intervals. Later, the spaces in between these forts were filled with ramparts to form the Antonine Wall. The fort at the western end of the wall was near Dumbarton. This fort and the ford across the then-shallow River Clyde from Dumbuck was given further protection by the establishment of a fort or camp, Vanduara, near Paisley. Ptolemy's map of around 141AD shows Vanduara. The main Roman road running up the west of Britain reached the Clyde where Glasgow now stands, forded the river and went on to Vanduara.

The Military Way ran parallel to the wall 50 yards south of it. It was linked to an elaborate system of roads, forts and fortlets and, since part of the Roman army's food supply came to Caledonia from depots in the south, it is more than likely that a road ran from the ford at the Clyde to meet this network and so reach the western end of the wall at Dumbarton.

Such a road would, for safety, have run along the north bank of the Clyde, and thus over the Kelvin. Standing on Yorkhill, one can see how splendid a vantage point the hill is, and it seems likely that the Romans would have placed an outpost of Vanduara here, overlooking the lower reaches of the Clyde and Kelvin. It would have protected a crossing over the Kelvin and under its protection people would have gathered and built dwelling places.

Thus far is speculation, but at Yorkhill in 1867, while a new garden was being prepared, some Roman remains were uncovered. These included a brass coin of the Emperor Trajan (98-117AD), a bronze and a silver coin, a bronze or copper ring and a large bronze thumb ring, eleven fragments of four separate vessels, fragments of part of a small vase and a quantity of wheat similar to that issued to Roman military stations. As wheat did not grow in Caledonia at that time it would have been imported. These finds were displayed in the Glasgow Exhibitions of 1888 and 1901.

So we move from the realm of possibility to that of probability, and can assume that dwelling places were established at the River Kelvin near Yorkhill in Roman times, if not before. A little further north an old road ran along the north-east side of Dowanhill until about 1800. Known as the Roman Road, it may have run from the Kelvin to the fort at Bearsden or at Balmuildy as part of the Roman network of roads.

The Kingdom of Strathclyde:

After the Romans left Caledonia early in the 5th Century AD, a series of small kingdoms sprang up including Strathclyde, with Dumbarton as its capital. Protected by successive fortresses built on Dumbarton Rock, it was an important town commanding the mouth of the Clyde.

Around 1180 Jocelyn wrote in his *Life of St. Kentigern:* 'King Rhydderch remained longer than usual in the royal town which is called Pertnech.' Rhydderch Hael became ruler of Strathclyde in 550AD and it was he who invited Kentigern to return from Wales. Some historians assert that Rhydderch died in the Royal House de Perthec in 603. However, no records of Partick have yet been found which date from the period between the time of his death and 1136, when King David granted Partick to the Bishop of St. Kentigern's Church.

So for centuries, the road from Glasgow to Dumbarton via Partick was a highway of some importance, although in 1818 there were only three villages on this road, apart from a few houses at Anderston. These were Partick (with a ferry to Govan), Yoker (with a ferry to Renfrew) and Kilpatrick. The only river of any consequence the road crossed was the Kelvin, and at some time a bridge was built over it. Around the bridge and its toll, inns and alehouses were established and the village of Partick came into being. The first stage of its history to be found on record starts with the grant of Partick by David to the Bishop of St. Kentigern's Church. The Bishop erected a mill on the Kelvin at Partick to serve Glasgow.

The bishops:

The history of Glasgow before the 12th century is no longer on record, because at the Reformation James Beaton, the last Roman Catholic Archbishop of Glasgow, fled to France taking with him the records of the See. These were deposited in Paris at the

Scots College and with the Carthusians, but almost all of the large number of original charters disappeared during the French Revolution.

However, we know that on 7 July 1136, King David of Scotland granted lands at Perdeyc to the church of St. Kentigern at Glasgow (Glasgow Cathedral) at its dedication.

In 1147 King David granted Govan to the See of St. Kentigern, and soon afterwards Bishop Herbert made the Church of Govan a prebendary of the Cathedral. The gift also included the islands between Govan and Perthec*, together with that part of Perthec which the same king later gave to Bishop John and his successors, i.e. the lands of Perthec on the west of the Kelvin.

In 1161 Walter Fitzalan, ancestor of the Stewarts, was invited to Scotland by David and made High Steward. The vast grants of land he received from David included the whole of the area that later became Renfrewshire. As holder of the same office under Malcolm the Maiden, he received the part of Perthec that David had kept in his own hands.

But what was meant by the word Perthec and what area did it cover? It would seem that Perthec (almost certainly the same as the earlier Perdeyc) lay on both sides of the Kelvin, unlike the Burgh and District, which were only on the western side of the river, as was the village of the early 1800s.

James White claims that Perthec stretched as far east as Shettleston Cross. When he took over the Mill of Partick from his father in 1882 he began to look into its history, and his results were printed in the Glasgow Herald as four articles, issued in book form in 1934 under the title *Foundations of Glasgow*. He states that, prior to the Reformation, the Barony and Regality of Glasgow had five districts: City of Glasgow; Partick Ward; Govan Ward; Cadder Ward; and part of Monklands. He then states that these were altered in 1773 to: City of Glasgow; Barony Parish; Govan Parish; Cadder Parish; and part of Monklands. This suggests that the area covered by the Barony was the same as that covered by Partick.

When Rutherglen was made a Royal Burgh around 1126 it was granted certain rights over large tracts of land, one of which was described as 'from Kelvin to Garin' (Garrion, near Dalserf). This made the Kelvin the western boundary for Rutherglen, and thus the Lands of Perthec were divided into two parts. The principal part was east of the Kelvin. The other part, over which Rutherglen had no rights, was west of the Kelvin in Govan Parish. (In connection with this, it is interesting that on 3 June 1718 the inhabitants of Rugland (Rutherglen) were freed from paying any tolls at Partick bridge, which connected these two parts.)

On becoming a Bishop's Burgh in 1181, Glasgow wanted to be free of Rutherglen, but it was 1226 before Rutherglen lost its rights and privileges over the lands of Perthec from the Kelvin to the Cross of Shettleston.

The Manor House of Perthec:

In June 1362 a dispute between the Bishop of Glasgow and his Chapter was submitted for arbitration before the Bishops of Glasgow and Dunblane, at the Manor of the Bishop of Glasgow. The arbiters, as entered in the Registrum, were the Bishops of Argyll, Brechin, Dunkeld and Whithorn plus the Abbot of Holyrood. Others say the Bishop of Orkney was present.

---

*A map, published by Bleau in 1654, shows several islands or inches in the Clyde, which have since become joined to either the north or the south bank. The White (Whyt) Inch was joined to the north bank forming Whiteinch and the Clydeholm Shipyard of Barclay, Curle was later built on it. The Water Inch, at the mouth of the Kelvin, was also joined to the north bank and the Meadowside Shipyard of Tod & McGregor was built there.

It must have been an extremely important meeting for these bishops to have come from all over Scotland, and White draws two conclusions from its being held. Firstly, that the Manor was of considerable size, because of the number of people involved; secondly, that it was close to the Cathedral, because 'sundry conferences were held between so many important personages between the Cathedral Church of Glasgow and the Manor House of Perthik'.

This now links up with confusion surrounding Partick Castle. Most commentators say that the Manor House of the Bishop was at Perthec at the Kelvin, and that the arbitration of 1362 took place there. White disagrees and states that the Manor House of Perthec was beside the Cathedral in Glasgow. It is difficult to disagree with White, since it is not likely that such a large gathering of dignitaries and their attendants would travel from the Cathedral to the Kelvin; a rather long way with primitive transport on primitive roads. Six or seven important bishops plus their entire retinues could amount to over two hundred people, and it is difficult to imagine this number being accommodated in a summer residence on the Kelvin.

According to White, names found in the Glasgow Registrum and the Paisley Registrum between 1175 and 1262 include: Arnald de Perthec; Helia de Perthec; Walter, son of Arnald de Perthec; Domino Petrus de Perthec and Iohanne de Perthec. The Rector of the Church of Rutherglen was Philip de Perthec. He was followed by Domino Iocelin de Perthec, who was Canon of Glasgow in 1228. The last one is a lady named Cecilia, sister of William de Kathkert, and the widow of John de Perthec. White concludes that 'the Manor House de Perthec of William Lord Bishop of Glasgow of 1362 was on the lands of Perthec and situated not far from the Cathedral.' He calls this the Bishop's Castle and maintains that it and the Cathedral were opposite Provand's Lordship, in present-day Castle Street. He says that the Bishop had another house outwith the castle as a manorial residence, the "Bishop's Castle" on the Kelvin. White quotes specific entry numbers from the Registrum for his information, so his conclusions must be treated with the greatest respect.

Having chosen which version is the more convincing, there is still a problem. If, as seems likely, the early name of Partick referred to this very extensive area, why did the name end up attached to a small village beside the Kelvin? Why is there no vestige of the name anywhere else in such a large area? Could it be that when the town's mill was built on the Kelvin, it had the name the Mill of Perthec, meaning 'the mill belonging to Perthec', and that in time this came to be taken to mean 'the mill at Perthec' and thus the name came to be applied to the village beside the mill, i.e. in effect, the village got its name from the mill, and not the other way round? However, this theory does not explain how the name disappeared from the remainder of the old Perthec.

Partick Castle:

There are many references to a Partick Castle, but there seem to have been two buildings: the castle of the Bishops and the house of George Hutcheson.

The Bishops had a summer residence in Partick from before 1277 until the Reformation of 1560. This must have been a sizeable building as the Bishop would not travel without a large retinue of men: clerics, servants and men-at-arms. Its exact site is unknown; as is its fate. One old record says 'It is supposed to have stood on the bank which overlooks the junction of the Kelvin and the Clyde'. Such a manor would have brought people to settle about it hoping for employment or alms, as well as protection, and along with the mills it would have helped to establish a village on the west bank of the Kelvin close to the Clyde.

The ruin that was popularly known in the village as Partick Castle was in reality a country residence built by George Hutcheson, a Glasgow businessman who founded Hutcheson's Hospital in Ingram Street. This residence was situated south of Meadow Road (Castlebank Street) on slightly raised ground opposite the foot of Anderson Street. The contract between Hutcheson and Wm. Miller, a Kilwinning mason, for building the castle was dated 9th and 14th July 1611, and still existed in 1894. The castle was inhabited until about 1770, but in 1783, as it was roofless and in ruins, some of the stones were taken by the laird of the nearby Merklands Farm to build a house.

It is possible that when he built the house for Hutcheson, the mason used stones from the old Bishop's Castle, leading to the new building being dubbed Partick Castle. Alternatively, it may have received its name because of the choice of site. All traces of castle, manor and farm have vanished and our only references are the modern street names of Merkland Street and Castlebank Street. Little is known about the subsequent owners of the castle, although Napier states that the house was inhabited about 1770 by 'common tradespeople, who let out the upper floor for dancing'. Around this time the orchard and fields at Meadowside became a printfield and then the site of the Meadowside Shipyard in 1844. The Castle Green, between the stepping stones and the ford, became a commercial bleachfield and large works were built on it in 1824. Two businesses were later created on the site of the castle: the Partick Foundry, beside the river, and the Castlebank Laundry, north of the foundry.

Partick around 1650:

A map of Glasgow c1650 includes Partick and shows the western boundary of Glasgow to be St. Tennoch's Bridge (at about Oswald Street), with two roads leading west from it north of the Clyde and meeting near the present Art Galleries. These roads ran in the line of Sauchiehall Street and Argyle Street, passing only a few houses before reaching Partick. The main highway from the Bishop's Castle in Glasgow to his castle in Partick had a by-road (Finnieston Street) leading to the Clyde; the wooden cross near it gave the area the name of Stobcross.

Meadow Road, Byres Road, the Knowe, the Goat and the mills were all in the village in the Westsyde of Partik, west of the Kelvin. The Eastsyde of Partik included areas no longer thought of as being in Partick: the area now occupied by the Western Infirmary and the University of Glasgow was called the Auld Park of Partik, while that occupied by the Art Galleries was the New Park. The more northerly of the two westbound roads passed just in front of this as Partik Lone. It has been said that Newtoun was the new town of Partick. Glasgow was very small at this time, and as the Clyde was extremely shallow, with mid-stream islands from Saltmarket to Yoker, ships could not sail up to it and Irvine became its port. In 1668 Port Glasgow was developed and trade increased, but by 1770 Greenock began to overshadow it, so Glasgow began dredging the Clyde, making it navigable to large ships and resulting in a more rapid development of the city. This also transformed Partick from a village into a town, and led to the development of Whiteinch as a community.

PARTICK VILLAGE

The village after 1800:

Having crossed the River Kelvin, people travelling west from Glasgow in the early 1800s would find themselves entering the village of Partick. In *Glasgow and its Clubs*, Strang describes the village as it was in 1810:

> Among the many rural villages which at one time surrounded Glasgow, perhaps none surpass Partick in beauty and interest. Situated on the banks of a limpid and gurgling stream which flows through the centre, and beautiful as it was of yore with many fine umbraceous trees and above all ornamented with an old hoary castle, with whose history many true and many more fabulous tales are associated, and when to these were added its dozen or two comfortable, clean cottages and its picturesquely planted mills historically linked with the generous gift of the successful opponent of the lovely Mary at Langside, all combine to render the locality one of the most favourite of suburban retreats.

In his history, Napier gives a more detailed description of the village in the early 1800s. He explains that having reached the present Radnor Street, travellers could enter the village by one of two roads. They could go straight on along New Dumbarton Road, now the part of Argyle Street between the Art Galleries and the Kelvin Hall, which would take them to Partick Cross over the narrow 1797 bridge, still standing beside the main road bridge. At the time, this was still a country road with Mr. Bogle's mansion crowning the Gilmorehill estate on the right. On the left side was the Bishop's Road (Queen/Thurso Street) along which the Bishop used to pass on his way from the Cathedral to his castle.

A little farther on at Partick Cross, three cottages stood on each side at the foot of Byres Road. From here to Peel Street the only houses among the trees on the north side were the large mansions of Dowanhill House, Stewartville House and Muirpark House, with their porter lodges at the foot of avenues leading from Dumbarton Road.

North of Muirpark was Partickhill with its villas, and about a quarter of a mile further west were the grounds of Thornwood with its mansion on the summit of the hill and porter lodge on the road almost opposite Granny Gibb's cottage. This whole section of Dumbarton Road was lined with dykes or hedges, except for the mansion houses which had wooded policies. The old quarry where Partick Cross subway stands had a sawpit and a woodyard opposite it. Some time later Dowanvale House was built behind it.

The other way into Partick was along Old Dumbarton Road, which led to the south end of the old stone bridge from where travellers could either pass down Ferry Road or cross the bridge to the village. Lined with thatched cottages on both sides, (Old) Dumbarton Road ran northwards to Partick Cross. This part was later named (Partick) Bridge Street and the cottages on the east side were taken down when St. Peter's (Simon's) Church was built. From the Cross, the road ran west as the Turnpike Road (Highway to Dumbarton), which, rather than going through the heart of the village, was a sort of by-pass road taking traffic north of the village.

The main east-west road running through the village was the Meadow Road (now Castlebank Street). From the north end of the bridge, the Knowe Brae, with a row of small houses lining its eastern side, led to the Meadow Road. These houses ran northeast to Partick Cross via Coopers Well Road, on the northern side of which were three small thatched houses, with Barr's school in the centre.

Opposite the head of the Knowe stood a two-storey thatched house belonging to Allan Craig. Between this house and a row of buildings owned by James Craig stood a low thatched building which was used as a barn or potato house. It had a close running through it leading to some weavers' houses and shops. The house was known as Parliament House and the close as Parliament Close, because the weavers met there to discuss all kinds of questions. The names date to the time of the French Revolution.

The Knowe Brae was home to old-fashioned vegetable gardens, with pigs and hens, and these gardens sloped down to the Kelvin where the disused Caledonian Railway station is now. From Meadow Road two paths sloped down to a ford across the Kelvin, the Horse Brae and the Kilbrae. At the top of the Kilbrae, travellers could cross the Meadow Road, continue north up the Goat, and then on up the hill to Hyndland via the Coarse Loan (Hyndland Street).

The Goat (now Keith Street) was the centre of the village, and running from the east side of its foot was a row of houses raised a little above the level of the street. The police station was at the south-west corner.

From the Horse Brae westwards travellers would pass small houses which carried on printing operations in connection with the bleaching works, built on the old bleaching green of the castle. Opposite these were some thatched houses, one of which was home to Dr. Neil's school for small children. Almost opposite was Merklands Farm, the west boundary of which was Steps Road, leading to stepping stones over the Kelvin. A little farther west on the north side of the Meadow Road near the foot of the Cow Loan three thatched cottages marked the western boundary. Here travellers could go along a country road to what was long-known as Sandy Road, and thence to the main road to Dumbarton.

Hyndland Street, Partick.

Another old road from Glasgow Cathedral to Partick was formed by Bishop Dobbie. It ran from the Cathedral to Byres Road via a track later known as Dobbie's Loan. At its western end this became University Avenue. Until 1839 when Great Western Road was formed, Byres Road only went as far northwards as the present Hillhead Library before veering west across Horselethill towards Kirklee.

Employment:

Weaving was the trade of the majority of the villagers, while bleaching and printing were also early occupations. The following quote is taken from the Glasgow Mercury, 8 December 1789:

> To be let, for such a number of years as may be agreed upon, that Printfield situated in the village of Partick, on the bank of the Kelvin, having a beautiful south aspect, with the printing, boiling and dyeing houses, and other buildings, and a convenient dwelling house, nearly finished, consisting of a dining room, bedroom, closet and kitchen on the first flat, and two bedrooms and closet above, all as at present possessed by Mr. William Ewing. Apply to William Robb, the proprietor, at Meadowside, Partick.

Early in the 1800s George McFarlane, who succeeded Mr Ewing as owner of the bleaching works, erected a large four-storey building for printing and dyeing calico. In 1824 John Walker purchased the ground and buildings and erected extensive works for bleaching and finishing. He then let the other buildings to the Lancefield Spinning Co. as a power-loom factory. The establishment of the weaving factory and the bleaching works provided a stimulus for speedy development of other industry in the area.

The Spinning Company employed 160 people, with the men being paid £1 per week and the women from 5/6d to 9/6d. 180 people worked in the printfield and 82 in bleaching. There was also a good deal of hand-loom weaving carried on. A number of other villagers must have found work with the local flour, waulk and slit mills which were also right on their doorsteps.

In addition to these industries, coal had been dug for many years one and a half miles north of the ferry (according to the Statistical Account for the Parish of Govan in 1794). At Jordanhill and Cartnavel (sic), there were sixteen beds of coal ranging from three inches to two feet thick. Two of these were worked, as well as a large ironstone layer. With coal seams on Gilmorehill, it has been stated that 'the whole of the Byres Road district is honeycombed with old coal workings'. These, plus the farms and local quarries, must also have provided employment for some villagers.

Turkey red:

Turkey red (Adrianople Red) was a vivid dye, with the particular merit of being very fast. Applied to cotton only, it was used successfully in Scotland for 150 years. For a considerable time the process was kept secret, and dyeing became one of the city's biggest industries.

According to Napier, 'Glasgow has long acquired a name in the markets of the world for her printed handkerchiefs and shawls, the first of which were printed at Gilmourholm in 1754. Not long after this, turkey-red was being dyed in another field on the Kelvin Meadowside, by Papilon [sic]; '...the celebrated Papilon, who introduced Turkey Red dyeing into this country, had this field [in Partick] for a short time and during his possession it was burned and we do not think that he continued in it after.' However, David Dale and Geo. McIntosh engaged Papillon, the French turkey-red dyer, to set up the first British Turkey Red dyeworks - Dalmarnock Turkey Red Works at Barrowfield - some time after 1754. Scotland, if not Partick, introduced turkey red dyeing into Britain.

The Partick drum (now in the People's Palace):

The Partick drummer served as a kind of town crier, announcing public matters after attracting people's attention by beating his drum. Until the mid-1880s, he was heard every day in Partick at 5a.m. and 9p.m., setting the time of rising and going to bed, since there were few clocks at that time. The evening drum also acted to mark a kind of curfew, since it was not safe to be out after dark, there being little or no street lighting.

The drummer was elected at a public meeting and was paid by a contribution made at New Year. He charged a fee to make a public announcement, and this stood at 6d, rising to 9d and then 1/- as the village grew in size. The villagers provided him with a cloak for protection during wet weather, and around 1818, to avoid damage to the drum when it rained, he used a long tin trumpet morning and evening, ringing a bell during the day.

The evening tattoo finished in 1830 and the morning one in 1845, but public announcements were still made by the drummer up until 1855. At the back of the bleachworks on Castlebank Street there was a powerloom weaving mill run by the Lancefield Spinning Company. They employed a young man to sound a bugle through the village every morning at 5.30 in case any of their workers had missed the regular drum call at 5 a.m. Later, the shipyards had horns for a similar purpose.

In August 1853 (under the Burgh) the official method of announcing a meeting of householders to discuss acceptance of Burgh boundaries was by posting handbills 14 days before the meeting, by placing notices in the papers and by Tuck of Drum two days in each week for two weeks before the meeting. According to Greenhorne 'the Drum [now in the People's Palace] was presented to the Old Partick Club by Mr. Robert Napier, son of Mr. James Napier, F.C.S.' However, the Burgh minutes of July 1890 reveal that 'a letter was received by the Commissioners from Robert Robertson, carpenter of Bridge Street, asking whether they would accept a present from his wife of the old drum which had been used formerly in the Burgh to waken the citizens in the mornings. The offer was accepted.'

The Partick bell:

Another old custom involved the ringing of a bell at funerals and to announce the death of a villager. Shortly before the funeral, the town crier went through the village inviting everyone to attend, and people generally left their work and went without any formal dress. The custom prevailed in Partick until about 1780. Burials usually took place in Govan or Anderston.

The bell has a crest on it with the old bridge across it, and the date 1726 above it. It has an open iron handle for ease of carrying and ringing. It vanished for a time, then around 1870 a Mr. Ross bought it from a Paisley man. He had got it from a Glasgow broker who had bought it at a sale in Edinburgh. Mr. Ross presented the bell to the Partick Curling Club to be held pro tem.

PARTICK BURGH

Formation of the Burgh:

From being a small village in the early 1800s, Partick grew in size until it had become a small town by the 1850's.

The town was an increasingly popular residential quarter for wealthy city merchants, who erected houses north of the village in Dowanhill and Partickhill. But the main cause of Partick's growth was the establishment of the shipbuilding yards. By 1850, Tod & McGregor's Meadowside Yard was set up on the west bank of the Kelvin, and in 1863 the Pointhouse Yard of A. & J. Inglis was established on the east bank. To house the great influx of workers arriving from all over Scotland and Ireland, large tenement blocks were built and a transport system developed to carry them to their workplaces either side of the Clyde.

Partick's expansion brought social problems in the form of rowdiness, drunkenness and 'corner boys' (young men who congregated at street corners with little to do). Additionally, the large and vociferous section of the community who espoused the Orange cause deeply resented the smaller group of recently arrived Irish Catholics. Other problems caused by expansion included the health hazards of open drains, middens and piggeries. Ditches and burns were used as sewers, leading to repeated outbreaks of fevers and cholera.

As a result of several acts of violence that had occurred during the winter months - especially near the new bridge over the Kelvin - some gentlemen in and around the village started to put up street lamps in 1844. The management of these matters was in the hands of a committee selected by those who had subscribed to the scheme, the understanding being that each one would pay 6d per £1 of rental (similar to modern building rates).

The scheme was a success, and the number of lamps was gradually increased until by the time the committee applied to become a burgh, they had erected 99 lamps and lighted part of the Dumbarton Turnpike Road from the bridge over the Kelvin on the east to the lands of Whiteinch on the west. They had also put numerous lamps on Partickhill, Crow Road and many other roads.

In order to be declared a burgh, application had to be made to the Sheriff of Lanarkshire giving due cause, and demonstrating the intention of the citizens to accept the responsibilities that the change would give rise to. Under the Police Act a burgh had powers to raise money to watch, light, clean, drain and pave its own localities.

On the 12th November 1851 a meeting was held in Mr. Shanks's schoolroom to discuss the situation. The Inspector of the Poor for Govan Parish, who dealt with complaints about nuisances, had agreed to meet the ratepayers. So a committee was chosen to consult the unfeued proprietors, and it reported back in March 1852 that there was little probability of these proprietors agreeing to carry out any joint drainage system voluntarily. Instead, application was made to have the General Police Act of Scotland adopted by the households of the locality, whereby the payment of rates could be made compulsory.

Three months later the Sheriff gave approval to their petition to constitute themselves into a burgh under the management of twelve commissioners, three of whom would be magistrates. In July 1852, at a public meeting in the Free Church schoolroom, a motion for the adoption of the Act was carried unanimously and at the first council meeting on 9 August David Tod of Tod & McGregor was elected senior magistrate.

The first Commissioners were:

Moses Hunter	James Thomson	James Napier
John Walker jun.	Alexander Shanks	Robert Paterson
John White	Robert Kay	George Richmond
David Tod	John Buchanan	David Ralston

Tod became Provost, and, until the Burgh ceased to exist in 1912, there were 15 Provosts of Partick:

David Tod	1852-7	Andrew McLean	1883-91
John White	1857-60	James Caird	1891-8
Robert Robinson	1860-3	Alexander Wood	1898-1902
Allan Arthur	1863-9	William Kennedy	1902-5
Robert Hunter	1869-72	John White, jun	1905-8
George Thomson	1872-5	Thomas Logan	1908-11
John Ferguson	1875-8	Thomas Stark Brown	1911-12
Hugh Kennedy	1878-83		

Provosts numbers 2 and 13 were father and son.

The commissioners first met in Partick Academy (Church Street), where they were given the use of rooms until more suitable accommodation could be acquired. Later, they met in the Police Buildings until the Burgh Halls were erected in 1872.

In April 1869 the Burgh was divided into four wards. After some time it was re-divided into five, and in 1902 into six wards. (Under the re-organisation of 16 May 1975, Strathclyde Regional Council was formed. The wards were reduced to two, viz. Partick East and Partick West).

In 1872 the grounds of the University and of the Western Infirmary, which up until then had been included within the second ward, were annexed to the City of Glasgow by an Act of Parliament; despite the strenuous opposition of the Burgh, which presented a financial claim against the City in the following year.

At first the Burgh was run by a Commission with Commissioners, but as a result of the Town Councils (Scotland) Act of 1900, it was administered by a Town Council with Councillors after 31st. December 1900.

The Commissioners' meetings were for many years very largely taken up with transforming the village into a town. Much had to be done and the first piece of business each year after the elections was to assess the citizens for rates to pay for improvements. The biggest task was the laying of a sewer system into which were incorporated the River Kelvin and the various burns in the Burgh.

Throughout the life of the Burgh, many problems had to be addressed and the Commissioners, and later the Councillors, applied themselves diligently to the tasks of establishing public services and adapting them to cope with the ever-changing demands of modern life. Roads were taken over and made public, having been given good surfaces and supplied with pavements. Old thoroughfares were widened to cope with the ever-increasing volume and weight of traffic. Many had to be altered again when the railways were introduced.

Lamps were erected in the streets, along with street name-plates and numbers on tenement closes. Streets were dug up to lay lines for the tramcars, and poles erected to carry the overhead trolley wires. A Police Force and a Fire Brigade were formed and their premises, uniforms and equipment all had to be supplied and wages negotiated.

Vigilance had to be exercised to keep infections from turning into epidemics. Tuberculosis, scarlet fever, diphtheria, measles and whooping cough were all dealt with while typhoid and cholera were an ever present threat. Strict regulations needed to be applied to dairies and slaughter-houses to maintain a safe level of hygiene. Partick was ahead of its time, and in 1852 appointed an Officer of Health who doubled as Police Surgeon. A hospital was also needed, especially after the Public Health Act of 1867 when Glasgow refused to take patients from nearby burghs.

During the life of the Burgh a great many bye-laws and regulations were laid down to control the running of the Burgh in a competent manner. Subjects included Hackney Carriages and Drivers, Common Lodging Houses, Stair-Cleaning, Porters, Coal Porters, Chimney Sweeps, Public Parks, Fire Brigade, Milk Supplies and a host of others, all of which kept the various committees very busy.

The population of the burgh increased rapidly, and overcrowding was reported by 1864.

The late 1870s were troubled times. In July 1877 there was destitution due to a lock-out in the shipyards. In November 1878 there was an epidemic of scarlet fever, at its worst in Whiteinch. There were 48 deaths during this month, 19 in December, and it was February before the epidemic finally finished. In 1879 the Partick Relief Fund for the Deserving Unemployed gave soup and bread to over 800 people in January, and to 900 in February. Coal was distributed to many people and lines were handed out to be given to grocers in return for provisions in cases of great need.

The Burgh coat of arms:

The Commissioners approved the armorial design in February 1872. The images in the four quarters were as follows:

ARMORIAL BEARINGS
of the
BURGH OF PARTICK.

1st and 4th: OR. A Lymphad or Galley with oars in action.

2nd: GULES. A castle with two circular towers ARGENT, masoned SABLE.

3rd: GULES. A Bishop's mitre, proper and on a second of the chief a Garb or Wheat Sheaf, between two millstones of the first.

The burgh motto is *Industria Ditat* - Industry Enriches.

A drawing of the coat of arms by the Partick architect Wm. Leiper was submitted in November 1869, although it is not clear whether he also designed it. The coat of arms reflects some of the history of Partick with references to shipbuilding, the wheat mills and the Bishop and his castle.

Features of Burgh life

Milk shops and dairies:

In 1872-3 164 people died in Partick during a smallpox epidemic. The major source of infection was the burgh's milk supply, in spite of the fact that byres were licensed and milkshops and dairymen registered. Even as late as 1904 Partick experienced an outbreak of enteric fever due to infected milk.

A Sanitary Report of 1886 gives a list of all the cowsheds, milk shops and dairies visited in the Burgh. There were 53 engaged in these branches of the milk trade and a very close watch was kept on them by the authorities to prevent the spread of infection. One report reads: 'There are 15 cowkeepers with a total number of 156 cows and the byres are clean and well kept.'

Milk was a potential source of tuberculosis, which was once common, especially in the form of consumption (pulmonary tuberculosis) and, as they used a lot of milk, a register of ice-cream shops was also kept. Similarly, a register of manufacturers of margarine, margarine-cheese and milk-blended butter was kept. Inspectors also checked that milk had not been watered down and that butter had not had margarine added to it.

Ice cream shops:

In the early 1900s a register was kept of these shops, as well as 'aerated water shops' which included greengrocers, fruiterers, milkshops, restaurants, confectioners, etc. The ice cream shops were all owned by Italians. A 1912 register of places for public refreshment listed ice cream shops, fish restaurants, newsagents and bakeries.

In 1911 one Reverend Gray gave an address to the Scottish Council for Women's Trades attacking the evils of these ice cream shops. He began, 'Let it be said at once that no indiscriminating or sweeping charge is brought against this whole class of shop. It is not implied that all or even a majority of those who keep them are men of unworthy character. ... [But] the way in which they are conducted and the hours during which they keep open become contributing causes in the downfall of many boys and girls, that a number of vicious practices are connected with them and that some of the men who keep them are men of evil character.'

Among the heinous things their clientele were accused of included staying in the shops until they closed at midnight, playing the gramophone, and playing dominoes or cards for halfpenny stakes. Sad to say, they had tamed down quite considerably by the time I started frequenting them.

Coal porters '...shall always be provided with a sufficient Stool, Basket or Creel, and Shovel.'
A table of fares was laid down for carrying Coal, Dross or Triping, Charcoal or Coke.

Porters:

Each porter had to wear a uniform cap with the words Partick Porter and his license number on the front and the same painted on each side of his barrow or hurley. Stations or districts were allotted to them, although the restrictions did not apply at flittings. No more than four were allowed at a station, and a table of rates was laid down. Amongst other things they carried letters and parcels.

Chimney sweepers:

It was specified that chimney sweepers must always be provided with sufficient ropes, ladders, bags, besoms etc. Different rates were paid for the sweeping of kitchen vents; room vents; shops, banks, warehouses and public offices; 'foul chimneys', and 'extra work'.

Stair cleaning:

Stairs in the tenements had to be swept every lawful day (every day except Sunday) and washed twice a week. 'No carpets, floor cloth, rug or mat shall be shaken or beaten from any window, flat, platform, close, stair or other height within the Burgh under any pretence whatever' read one stern warning. Carpets could be beaten in the back court but only between the hours of 7-9 from October to April, and 6-8 from April to October.

Partick's village origins:

Though a burgh, Partick, before the erection of the tenements, still retained many of the characteristics of a village. On Meadow Road, a row of two-storey houses stretched along the north side to Orchard (Vine) Street and, on the south side, from the Horse Brae to the Lancefield Weaving Factory. Similar houses existed on both sides of Dumbarton Road from Church Street to Byres Road. On Dumbarton Road west of Byres Road was the short Church Place leading to Partick East Church, then the Burgher Row (later Wallace Place) and west of that was the porter lodge of Dowanhill House. A boundary wall ran from this point to Stewartville House porter lodge, and another wall to the porter lodge of Muirpark House.

Two-storeyed houses were built in Bridge Street, the Goat and along Dumbarton Road westwards to the Cow Loan. The area from Hyndland Street to Peel Street was still countryside.

Towards the end of the nineteenth century Hayburn Street was just a country lane leading to a small dairy owned by Thomas Dunlop. On the eastern side of this lane was Hayburn Cottage and on the west, a villa, then a cottage and two other villas, all with front and back gardens. The two westmost villas were later taken down to make way for Rosevale Terrace. The stones were numbered and re-erected on a new site in Crow Road and named Beechcroft (425 & 427 Crow Road) and Emslie (431 Crow Road).

On the north side of Dumbarton Road east of Crow Road were villas called Greenbank, standing well back with large front gardens. Behind these were extensive nursery gardens covering the entire area that later became the railway depot, while to the east, Turnerfield Grove, surrounded by large trees and facing the Hay Burn (then an open stream as far down as Dumbarton Road) occupied ground later taken over by the North British Railway passenger station.

The building at the west corner of Crow Road and Dumbarton Road was Downie Place and beyond it were Meadowbank Place, Apsley House, Meadowbank Crescent and Maule Terrace. A series of well-built houses stood on the north side of Dumbarton Road running westwards to the estate of Thornwood.

After passing Crow Road, the only buildings on the south side as far as Whiteinch were Crawford Place, Fairfield, Sandbank Place, Granny Gibb's cottage and a two-storey tenement on the east side of Sawmill Road. Along the road stretching south to the Clyde was Merkland Farm, long occupied by a Mr McGavin.

Keith Street:

'These were weavers' houses built of brick, possibly from Messrs. Gilchrist & Goldie's Partick Brick Works in Crow Road and were demolished in the 1930s. The picture shows Miller's second-hand furniture shop. The pend, the only entry into the backyard, is the entranceway furthest away from the camera. Inside the pend, the entrance was about 15 steps up. On the common landing the occupiers shared a swan-shaped water tap, known throughout Partick as the Herry Well. In the backyard to the left was a joiner's shop and straight ahead a plumber's store. South of the wee white building stood Menzies, the bookshop [and newspaper] distributors, and the Partick smiddy. Immediately opposite the Head of the Goat there was a wafer biscuit factory (before the Sovereign Boot Company [was built]). During the winter the show people came to stay in their gypsy caravans [around here].

Farther down from Walker Street was the Mission Hall, later the Labour Exchange. It housed the 60th. Boys Brigade (Dowanhill Church). Next there was a small foundry, then the Quakers Burying Ground with houses to the rear with a spiral staircase and at the corner, Fleming's stableyard.

Heading towards Partick Cross, there was a lane where the juvenile football club, Partick Glencairn, had its clubroom. The triangle opposite the A.O.H. [Ancient Order of Hibernians] hall had a cast-iron fountain. The A.O.H. hall was built later, the site being known as the Gable End. The shows came there once a year with a boxing booth. In Well Street was a quack chemist, Wee McGregor. P.& R. Fleming, structural engineers, occupied the site at the foot of the Goat with their works for many years.' (reminiscence in the West End News)

Keith Street was formerly known as Kelvin Street

The surroundings of Dowanhill Church c1889:

In the *History of Dowanhill Church* we are given a description of the roads and buildings around this church, which is situated near the top of Hyndland Street at the gushet where Hyndland Road leads off to the left

Immediately to the east there were scarcely any houses at that time until one reached Byres Road - except for Elgin Terrace (at the west end of Havelock Street). There was no Dowanhill Park and no Dowanhill School. Foremount Terrace existed (at the west end of Highburgh Road), but Havelock Street, Alexandra (Elie) Street, the upper end of Dowanhill Street and most of Wood (White) Street, and Lawrence Street were yet to be built. The gushet at Byres Road and Church Street still had its old thatched cottages and little gardens with a piggery here and there.

To the north-east there were scarcely any houses in Hyndland Road - only West Lodge and Osborne Lodge, which stood untenanted for many years, plus a few tenements called Hillside Gardens, with Hyndland Station, Westbourne Terrace and Montague Terrace beyond the station. Lindsay's Farm still stood on the east side of Hyndland Road, almost opposite where Hillend Gardens stood.

Hyndland consisted of green fields for another ten years. The west side of Hyndland Street was only built up to the corner of White Street, which had only two tenements at the south-east end, called Beaconsfield Street. West of Hyndland Street and Beaconsfield Place a bare hillside stretched to the West of Scotland cricket ground.

A newspaper reported in June 1898: 'The Cross will be very much altered soon. At the Byres Road corner the British Linen Bank's handsome buildings are receiving the finishing touches while on the other side of the street those old buildings in the triangular piece of ground between Well Street and New Bridge Street (Benalder Street) are being demolished.'

By an Act of 1893 thatched roofs became unlawful, with a period of grace of seven years permitted for removal, although there were still three such roofs in Partick by 1900: one vacant house in Byres Road, and a byre and a workshop in Whiteinch. By 1900 there were no pig styes left in Partick.

On 29 June 1903 the Glasgow Citizen reported:

> The transformation of Partick goes on apace. The row of two-storey whitewashed dwellings extending from Church Street to Byres Road, a relic of old Partick, is now in course of demolition and the site will be occupied with a range of up-to-date houses. West of Byres Road the district has been greatly altered in appearance and several of the older buildings between that point and the North British Railway Station are scheduled to come down. Approaching Partick West a few of the remaining villas flanking Dumbarton Road are also being cleared away and new streets are being completed over the summit of Broomhill, a district which is rapidly becoming built-up.

...but a change of status was on the way.

The annexation battles:

During the 19th century Glasgow had been steadily swallowing up the burghs and villages on its borders. However, the battle to include Partick and Govan was protracted due to the opposition put up. Glasgow argued that the people who lived in the satellite burghs enjoyed the advantages of city life without paying city taxes. Also, as there was little building space left, Glasgow was losing its wealthier citizens as they moved to the suburbs.

In 1869 Bailie Hinshelwood brought the Representation of the People (Scotland) Bill to the attention of the Govan Commissioners, by which Glasgow hoped to annexe Partick and Govan. Both towns were greatly incensed and fought the Bill. A petition was signed by 1,000 citizens, and deputations went to London. After a long battle the two burghs triumphed and Glasgow was defeated.

In the following year Glasgow put another Bill through Parliament to annexe Govan, Partick, Hillhead and Maryhill but it was so unreadable it was rejected in the House of Commons on the second reading.

Two years later another Bill was promoted to annexe Alexandra Park, Springburn and a portion of the Burgh of Partick together with Govanhill and Queens Park. The Bill was passed so far as the first three districts were concerned, and Partick was given some compensation for loss of rateable value. (The portion of Partick was the part on which the University and the Western Infirmary stood. Some Glaswegians had been annoyed that technically Partick could claim to be a university town, whereas Glasgow couldn't).

In 1875 a third Bill was presented to include Crosshill, Govanhill, Queens Park, Pollokshields, Mount Florida and Polmadie within the Glasgow boundaries. This was rejected after a lengthy inquiry. In March of that year it was suggested that Partick, Hillhead and Maryhill unite to form one burgh which would have been too large to be threatened by the Glasgow, but the idea was shelved.

In 1879 a fourth Bill was put forward and rejected.

The foot of The Goat, looking west, showing the old police office.

Proposed extensions:

Though Partick vigorously opposed the plans to swallow it up, it did not turn down two expansionist moves on its own behalf.

In February 1881 the proprietor of the Kelvinside Estate applied to the Partick Commissioners to extend Partick Burgh to include Kelvinside District and thus form the Burgh of Partick & Kelvinside. This plan was mooted because drainage in the estate was inadequate and becoming too expensive to remedy. Partick petitioned the Sheriff for the extension arguing that, since its burgh boundaries had been drawn up, a large number of houses had been built just north of it and all the sewage from them passed through Partick. The new populous district lying between the northern boundary of the Burgh and Great Western Road drained into the sewer passing through Partick down Byres Road to empty into the large sewer built by the Commissioners from Dumbarton Road to the river. Gartnavel Asylum and houses in Kelvinside and Hyndland drained into the Hay Burn, an open water-run which had been converted into a large common sewer.

Therefore, it was proposed that Kelvinside district be included in the Burgh of Partick. At the same time Hillhead Burgh put forward a similar claim to include Kelvinside, but Glasgow objected to both schemes on the grounds that Kelvinside was not an outgrowth of either Burgh and again claimed that the city should be extended to include Partick and Hillhead. The feuars in Kelvinside objected to their proprietor's proposal and the Sheriff turned down the petitions of both Burghs.

At the time the Burgh of Hillhead was very small, comprising an area to the east of Byres Road as far as the Kelvin. Kelvinside, on the other hand, was considerably larger, stretching northwards on the west side of Byres Road from the Partick boundary as far as the Kelvin, which separated it from Maryhill. It also stretched as far westwards as Anniesland Toll (Cross) and Balshagray Avenue. The proposed joint Burgh would have been very large.

In 1900 Partick discussed with Renfrewshire the possibility of extending the Burgh boundary northwards from Crow Road at Jordanhill Station to Anniesland Toll; north along the county boundary to the north of the Skaterigg Brick Works; and westwards along the county boundary to the Joint Hospital and beyond. If this had been passed, Jordanhill and most of Scotstounhill would have been added to Partick Burgh.

In both 1883 and 1884 Glasgow submitted yet further annexation Bills, but Parliament affirmed that it would not annexe any community against its consent.

When yet another Bill was submitted in 1887, Govan was much handicapped by Plantation which wished to be included within the boundaries of Glasgow. Partick again clung to its independence, but in 1912 Glasgow was finally successful in bringing Partick and Govan within its boundaries, and the burghs became mere districts of Glasgow on 5 November 1912.

The end of the Burgh:

At midnight on 4 November 1912, the Burgh of Partick ceased to exist, and while the burgh organist played 'Lochaber No More', the Provost had the chain of office removed from his neck and his robe was laid aside. In December the gold chains and officials' badges of office were handed over to the Corporation for preservation in Kelvingrove Museum.

PARTICK DISTRICT

World War I:

The First World War started less than two years after Partick had been annexed by Glasgow, and although the district was well away from the field of conflict many of its citizens served on land and at sea. The yards in Partick built and repaired ships for the Royal Navy and the merchant fleet. Munitions works were set up on the Bunhouse Ground (later the site of the Kelvin Hall) in the building leased by the Glasgow Indoor Bowling and Recreation Company, Ltd. Called the Edith Cavell National Projectile Factory, it was run by Mechan's for the Ministry of Munitions. The wartime production targets brought about an influx of many 'key workers' resulting in a housing shortage, which in turn led to civil confrontation.

Between the wars:

After the war ended, Partick suffered as much as anywhere else in the 1920s and 1930s with the Depression, the General Strike of 1926, dole queues, the Means Test, and the Parish. Territorial gangs flourished in Glasgow, and the annual Orange Walk on the 12th of July resulted in many a running battle.

There was that strange experience each year on Armistice Day, 11 November, when all traffic stopped at 11 a.m. Every pedestrian stood to attention and not a person or vehicle moved for two minutes in memory of those killed in the war.

Shipyard horns boomed out their warning in the mornings to tell those who had work to get a move on, and the New Year was brought in with all the ships on the river sounding their horns.

Men singing in the backcourts for money or a 'piece' were common, as was door-to-door begging. Football continued to dominate the sporting interests of the men, and cinemas and dance halls flourished.

The large closely-packed tenement blocks began to deteriorate into slums, especially in the older property south of Dumbarton Road, where there were many 'single ends'. Most of these houses didn't even have their own toilet, there being a communal 'lavvy' (sometimes known as the 'closet' or 'cludgie') on the half-landing, serving all the houses on the level above. Chimneys continued to belch out smoke from their coal fires and deposited grime and soot on the buildings - and in people's lungs - and caused dense fogs from time to time.

There were pipe clay and clay pipes. The pipe clay was used when washing the stairs, and the clay pipes were for smoking tobacco or blowing soap bubbles, but oh so vulnerable when they were dropped on the ground.

Most houses had a sink at the window, a range for cooking, a coal bunker, and, just inside the front door, a hallstand for coats and hats. There were early wireless sets which succeeded the crystal sets with their 'cat's whiskers'. The wax cylinders of the primitive gramophones were replaced with new models which could only play one side of a record with their steel needles before needing to be wound up again; about three minutes playing time. Brass was very much in evidence, especially on the front doors of the houses and was polished vigorously with Brasso.

The character and class of the closes got fancier the further north one went from Dumbarton Road. Up the hill you started to get 'wally' closes with tiled walls, some with splendid designs. Further north still, the tiling was continued up the stairs to the first storey or even higher, and some had small gardens in front. At the foot of the hills the windows on the landings were of plain glass, but higher up among 'the toffs', they had decorated glass reminiscent of stained glass windows.

Streets had little traffic, mainly coalcarts pulled by large powerful Clydesdale horses, and lorries delivering milk and bread. This meant children could play in the side streets with reasonable safety. Football was played (except when the 'polis' appeared) with a tanner ba'; a small rubber ball which cost a tanner (sixpence). Using the small ball led to great dexterity of foot. Another game was 'wee heidies' (headers) against the wall with a tennis ball.

Children played a great variety of games on the pavements and sometimes on the nearly empty streets. Girls would play peever or 'beds' (hopscotch), moving a flat piece of marble or a flat tin skilfully with their feet, or they would play at skipping ropes, with a girl at each end cawing the rope, all of them singing out children's street rhymes. Both boys and girls played with peeries, little wooden spinning tops with the top surface brightly coloured with chalks, and made to spin by whipping with a piggy, made from a rolled up piece of cloth.

The foot of The Goat, looking east.

Boys could be seen playing in the gutter with bools (marbles) or playing moshie with them in the backcourts. They would run along the streets wheeling girds (iron hoops) propelled by a cleek, or walk balanced precariously on stilts formed from four pieces of wood or, more cheaply, from two tin cans and two pieces of string. Pedestrians at times had to dodge 'bogies' put together from pram wheels and an apple box. Among the more boisterous games were kick-the-can, leave-o and hunch-cuddy-hunch. Boys found lots to do in the back courts, climbing and jumping (and falling off) the dykes, (the brick walls dividing some of the backcourts), the roofs of the middens (ashpits) and wash-houses, stopping every so often to call up to the window of their houses, 'Mammy, throw me down a jeely piece!'

Some became painfully aware of just how dangerous were the spiked railings which fenced off some backcourts. Boys would slide down the banisters in the closes, though attempts were sometimes made to stop this by fitting small brass studs all the way along them. Cricket as well as football was played in the backcourts, with the stumps drawn on the wall in chalk. Every so often a craze would come into fashion (just like the hula hoops in later years) such as yo-yos and hi-li bats.

Boys collected the cigarette cards which some manufacturers put in the packets. These were designed in sets covering a wide range of subjects, with a coloured picture on one side and the relative information on the other. Girls collected dabbities and scraps. At certain times of the year, notably Guy Fawkes Night, wood and old furniture would be collected and a bonfire lit (illegally) at selected street crossings.

We had some moments of excitement such as when the ragman appeared with his horse and cart announcing his arrival with a bugle. We would run upstairs to plead for old rags, take them down and be rewarded with a balloon or a small celluloid windmill. Spirits rose in the hot weather when the water cart came sprinkling water behind it over the dusty streets. We loved to see cars ready to leave for a wedding and would run up to them with a cry of 'Hard up'. The occupants would throw out a handful of small coins as they left leading to a 'scramble' to collect them. Weddings and funerals were about the only time ordinary people saw the inside of a motor car. Mourners wore black arm bands or a curious little black diamond sewn on to a coat sleeve.

A great favourite with children (and their often sorely harassed parents) was going to the 'penny crush' matinees in the local cinema to watch the cowboys (look out behind you!), squirming with boredom when the hero and the heroine kissed and stamping and jeering when the film broke down.

There were no comfortable betting shops then, but back-close bookies and their runners. Those who could afford them took trips 'doon the watter'; to Rothesay and Dunoon, and also to the Ayrshire coast, with Ayr and Saltcoats as firm favourites.

There were no telephones in houses, and instead newspaper shops had a small blue plate hanging outside saying 'You may telephone from here'. It was before the age of the vacuum cleaner, and people went down to the backcourt to hang their carpets over the railings and get to work with a cane beater. There were no refrigerators, and milk turned sour quickly in very hot weather. In those days the obsession with selling foodstuff in impenetrable wrappings had not arrived - paper pokes were the order of the day, and there was not a poly bag in sight. Most commodities were sold loose, resulting in a certain percentage being damaged and sold off cheaper; such as broken biscuits and chipped fruit.

Shopping was altogether different then, with no supermarkets but a host of small grocery chains, such as Cochrane's, Massey's and Templeton's. Service was slower as there were a lot fewer items pre-packed. A large barrel-shaped mound of butter sat behind the counter and your order was taken off it with two wooden pats which shaped the butter before it was wrapped. Cheese was cut from a similar mound by means of a cutting wire. Eggs were sold loose and an electric light bulb was used for testing whether the egg was fresh. Bacon was sliced with a knife as it was some time before slicing machines were generally installed. The range of fruit and vegetables was smaller in those days without the wide variety of exotic items available in the large supermarkets of today. Buy a bottle of sherry then, and it was wrapped in brown paper and tied it up with string.

There were no washing machines and few baths, and instead people went to the 'steamie' - the public washhouse and baths in Purdon Street. Wringers and mangles were used to squeeze the water out of the clothes.

Children had no television sets, videos, or computer games and boys had to wear short trousers into their teens. Many wore 'tackety buits' - heavy boots whose soles were covered with metal studs. Those who were unfortunate enough to be 'on the parish' wore ill-fitting suits of extremely coarse cloth, and often sported a most unusual haircut, with all their hair shaved off except for a tuft at the front.

In the public parks there were notices saying 'Keep Off the Grass' and the parkie blew his whistle if you did not obey. When a tramcar broke down we would excitedly run down to the bottom of the street and walk along Dumbarton Road counting all the trams held up by it. There were long summer holidays from school which were always sunny - at least in our memories - with the tar melting in the streets and sticking to our hands and clothes.

We smoked cinnamon sticks, imagining the day when we would dare to buy a single Woodbine and a match and smoke in the darkness of the cinema. Our favourite sweets were dolly mixtures, toffee balls, large buttermilk dainties in their green wrappers, sherbet dabs, liquorice allsorts, Highland Toffee, Palm Toffee and lucky bags. It was a different life for youngsters in those days, mostly happy, although less so for our parents who struggled along on so little money. But we were too young to know, and not knowing, we didn't care.

World War II

Those who lived through World War II will remember how it affected our lives: the identity cards, ration books, clothing coupons, queues at food shops, dried eggs, Spam, 'Air Raid Precautions', fire watchers, stirrup pumps for putting out fires, gas masks, and window panes criss-crossed with brown sticky paper in an attempt to stop flying splinters of glass caused by bomb blasts. There were heavy wooden beams to prop up closes if a bomb fell. Some closes had a baffle wall in front of them (made of brick with the ends painted white so as to be more easily seen in the black-out) to provide protection against blast and shrapnel. There were the black-outs (Put out that light!), and air raid shelters in the back-courts (sometimes put to more private uses!). There were emergency water stations all over Partick, with large pipes running from them along the gutters, and the long beams of the searchlights probing the night skies amidst the silver barrage balloons.

Perhaps the most memorable event for children was the Evacuation, when children and their mothers left Partick for areas safer than a shipbuilding city. Though war was not declared until Sunday 3 September, some children left on the previous day, when Dowanhill, Church Street, St. Peter's Boys, and St. Peter's Girls (the schools associated with Hamilton Crescent Clearing School) were evacuated from Partick Station. Most returned fairly soon.

Fathers, sons, husbands, brothers, volunteers and conscripts went off to war; many never to return. We sat around the wireless and listened to Lord Haw-Haw (Gairmany calling, Gairmany calling), to Workers' Playtime, Music While You Work and ITMA with Tommy Handley.

The chilling banshee wail of the air raid siren sounding the alert to signal a possible air raid stays in my memory, along with the welcome sound of the All Clear. Fortunately, most times that the sirens wailed no air raid occurred but on two particular occasions bombs were dropped on Partick. In the raid of 18 September 1940 Laurel Street, Crawford Street, Hayburn Street and the area south of Castlebank Street were all hit. But the most memorable and damaging was the 250lb H.E. bomb which dropped on the west basin of Yorkhill Quay.

H.M.S. Sussex

On 17 September 1940 this cruiser was berthed at Yorkhill Quay, ready to sail the next day after having had a turbine re-bladed. The work was a few days ahead of schedule and the crew had been recalled to join the ship at midnight. About 3 a.m. the following morning a German bomber dropped a 250 lb. bomb which crashed through the deck setting fire to the fuel and creating a threat to the ship's well-stocked magazine. Two crew members were killed and 29 injured. The bomb did not drop down the funnel as is so often claimed.

Emergency measures had to be taken immediately because there were over 2,000 people asleep near by, including the patients and staff of the Royal Hospital for Sick Children. As many as possible were hurriedly taken to parks and then to rest centres.

While this was going on, firemen made use of the Clyde ferry boats, the vehicular ferry with its elevating deck proving particularly useful. As the thick black clouds of smoke rose from the burning oil, the firefighters flooded the magazine as quickly as possible, for had it exploded, the devastation would have covered a large area. It took twelve hours to quell the fire and render the area safe, and it was two years before the Sussex could take to sea again.

This appears to have been a particularly unlucky incident, and since the Germans never referred to their success, it is probable that they did not know about it. Perhaps the plane was damaged and did not make it back to Germany.

The Blitz:

For two nights in March 1941 Clydeside was the target for German planes, and though Clydebank suffered the brunt of the attack, some bombs and land mines fell in and near Partick. The eastern part of Partick was rocked by the land mine(s) which landed damaging the bridge on Kelvin Way in the West End Park. The steeple of St. Enoch's church at the Old Dumbarton Road gushet suffered damage which later led to the building's demolition and replacement with a petrol station.

Much greater damage was done within Partick by a string of land mines which fell almost in line with the railway running northwards from Partickhill Station to Hyndland. The row of terrace houses on the west side of Peel Street overlooking the cricket ground received a direct hit and several houses were demolished, with fifty people being killed and eight injured. Two people were rescued alive after having been buried in the rubble for a week, but one subsequently died. Another mine struck a tenement on the north side of Dudley Drive killing thirty-six and injuring twenty-one. The section which was re-built can be seen clearly today.

At the western end of Partickhill Road three houses including the the manse of Dowanhill Church were destroyed, uncovering the long-hidden St. Blane's Well. The terrace opposite Notre Dame Convent was also hit. Although these incidents were serious in themselves, there was little bomb damage done in Partick apart from them.

PARTICK TODAY and TOMORROW

Partick had become a smokeless zone by 1975, allowing the authorities to begin to clean the surfaces of the tenements. The grime which had been deposited over the years was sand-blasted off to reveal the splendour of the red-sandstone buildings and the surprisingly light colour of the older grey ones. People could now see and appreciate the many long-hidden decorations incorporated in so many of the buildings.

There is no longer any resemblance to the old village, as so much of the burgh has altered. Only one flour mill remains by the Kelvin - the Scotstoun Mill on the west bank. The east bank is now a car park for the Museum of Transport. Dumbarton Road is still the main thoroughfare for traffic to and from Partick, although on crossing the bridge there is no longer a cobbled road with tram lines or overhead cables. Proceeding westwards, there are no tenements at the head of Thurso Street, no Standard Picture House, no police callbox at Partick Cross. The curved tenement with the pawnshop behind the police callbox has gone, and the site where the Western Cinema used to stand has been vacant for some years. Behind it, where the power sub-station used to stand, a building has been put up to house the Social Security offices which used to be in Peel Street.

The old house immediately west of the cinema is still standing and is called Partick Market. Next door to it, the F. & F. dance hall has become the Carlton F. & F. bingo hall and the row of shops west of it are still there unaltered. Round the corner on the east side of Keith Street is a public house, where the Subscription School stood in the days of the village.

The tenement between Mansfield Street and Hyndland Street has been taken down, and the site is now an open space where Partickonians can sit and watch the world go by. The character of some of the streets has been changed by No Entry signs and one-way traffic systems as announced in a newspaper article of October 1987:

> Horticulture is coming to Partick and in a big way. In a joint £80,000 project by Glasgow District Council, Strathclyde Region, the Housing Corporation and the S.D.A., eight major streets in the area are to be transformed with the planting of trees and plants. The work will basically involve resurfacing the road using block pavers and soft landscaping with trees and plant boxes. The idea is to improve the environment of the streets. At the moment the streets are very wide and largely tarmac. We also get a lot of through traffic from people travelling between Dumbarton Road and Byres Road. To reduce this traffic, we will be narrowing the carriageway, which will leave more room for pedestrians and landscaping. A one-way system will be introduced. The streets involved are Stewartville Street, Fordyce Street, Mansfield Street, White Street and Dalcross Street. The work is expected to be started in 1988.

This work is now completed, altering the appearance of the area for the better, with red bricks on the streets, decorative railings at the close-mouths and black, decorated bollards along the pavements.

The old Relief church has been demolished and the modern Partick South church erected to cater for several united congregations. Partick Housing Association has just built a new tenement in Dumbarton Road at the west corner of Anderson Street. There is no Partick Picture House in Vine Street, and although the subway station is still there it has been renamed 'Partick' now that it has a joint entrance with the railway station, which used to be on the north side of Dumbarton Road. On the south side of Dumbarton Road at the railway bridge the public toilet has been closed down, and a new one opened in Peel Street.

In Hayburn Street the old tram (later bus) depot now serves as a garage for vehicles belonging to the Regional Council. Hoey's is still on the corner and the Rosevale Cinema, which became a billiard club is now a supermarket. St. Mary's church has gone and has been replaced with flats. There are even flats erected inside the fence on the south side of the cricket ground.

As on many sites in Partick, new houses are being built, including ones on the west side of Peel Street where the terrace was hit by the land mine in the Blitz.

With the removal of the tenement on its the west side, Rosevale Street has been widened at the Dumbarton Road end so that, instead of being off-set, it is now directly opposite Crow Road, aiding the flow of traffic at this busy junction.

Further on, new houses have been built between Rosevale Street and Sandy Road, and the two railway bridges over Dumbarton Road at Thornwood are gone, leaving another open space where the citizens of Partick West can take their leisure.

Opposite this, the old Partick West railway station has been removed and in 1993 a new police station was built to replace the old building in Gullane Street. The latter is now closed and its future is uncertain.

Past Thornwood, on the south side of Dumbarton Road, is the site where Granny Gibb's cottage stood; once the centre of activity when the Highland drovers came to Partick. This has also become an important traffic point, where vehicles can join the Clydeside Expressway which carries large volumes of traffic at speed into Glasgow, by-passing the local roads. The expressway resulted in the removal of Meadowside Park and the Police Gymnasium. Between Dumbarton Road and Beith Street most of the old tenements have been pulled down, with new houses springing up to replace them. Even the Partick Fire Station has been converted to flats. Beyond this, the enormous building of the granary has two very large extensions alongside it.

The mills on the Kelvin, which initially led to the development of the village, were almost totally eclipsed by the shipyards which led to the development of the burgh. It is ironic to think that there is still a mill at Thurso Street while the shipyards have all vanished.

The greatest changes have probably taken place in Whiteinch, where many tenements blocks were removed to make room for the approach roads and flyovers in connection with the Clyde Tunnel, at the entrance to which there is now a 22-storey high-rise building in Curle Street.

In Partickhill, some of the old villas have been demolished to be replaced with modern flats and Partick now has a hotel, the Wickets, in Hamilton Crescent behind the cricket pavilion.

The future for Partick:

The Evening Times of 13 June 1990 reported 'a dramatic £280 million plan to create a Clydeside Riviera in Glasgow's West End.' Backed by Glasgow District Council, Strathclyde Region, the S.D.A. and the Clyde Port Authority the development, if it goes ahead, is to stretch from the Clyde waterfront to the gates of Kelvingrove Park. It is to include a waterfront park with shops, restaurants, a hotel, a maritime museum, a landscaped riverside walkway along the Kelvin leading past new houses, and office units. Also envisaged are a two-mile promenade along the Clyde to stretch from Yorkhill Quay to the Clyde Tunnel; a high-power business development centre to cater for 'smart' city companies; and a new community near the Kelvin Hall to be called Mill Village.

There is also provision for public open spaces including Kelvin Walk, Clyde Walk, Pointhouse Museum Park, Partick Waterfront Park and a variety of playgrounds, cycle and pedestrian paths. Kelvin Harbour, opening on to the Clyde, will boast restaurants, bars, shops and museum buildings set around a waterfront theme. Clyde Maritime say the project has been based around Partick's 800-year connection with shipping and the Clyde.

Many other features are mentioned for this highly ambitious scheme which is expected to be finished by the end of the century, although it is hard to see it being done in the present economic climate, especially as it would involve removing part of the expressway and building a high-level bridge where it crosses the river.

So Partick, which grew so quickly in the latter half of the 1800s, has now grown a little smaller with demolition of so many slum tenements. The oldest buildings still standing are the villas still left in Partickhill, the old police station, the school in Anderson Street and St. Simon's Church in Partick Bridge Street.

The oldest historical feature in Partick is the Quakers Burying Ground at the foot of Keith Street. It was presented to the village in 1733 by John Purdon, after whom the nearby street is named.

Virtually the whole of the old village south of Castlebank Street has been wiped out to make way for transport facilities; first the railway and now motor vehicles. The latter now present problems, with most streets lined on both sides with parked cars. In spite of the Expressway, Dumbarton Road has again become congested with vehicles, an unhappy concomitant of a thriving and vibrant community.

Dumbarton Road, c.1908